AF428257

To Sean & Minh,

You not only made this
possible, you made it fun

Look at the T-rex!
The biggest of all, she's a
microbiologist, expert on small

1

She studies
bacteria, viruses too
Her work might be helpful for
stopping the flu

2

She uses her tools, and always
is set
To search for the cures to
diseases you get

It's a very good thing she's a
hardworking sort,
This research is hard when
your arms are that short!

The brachiosaurus looks up
at the sky
To see if the day will be
wet or be dry
He studies how weather
progresses as well,

He's a meteorologist, couldn't you tell?

He makes his
predictions for sun,
rain, and snow
For hurricanes, floods,
and tornados, oh no!

On the news he
delivers the weather
with feeling
But being so tall he
must come through the
ceiling!

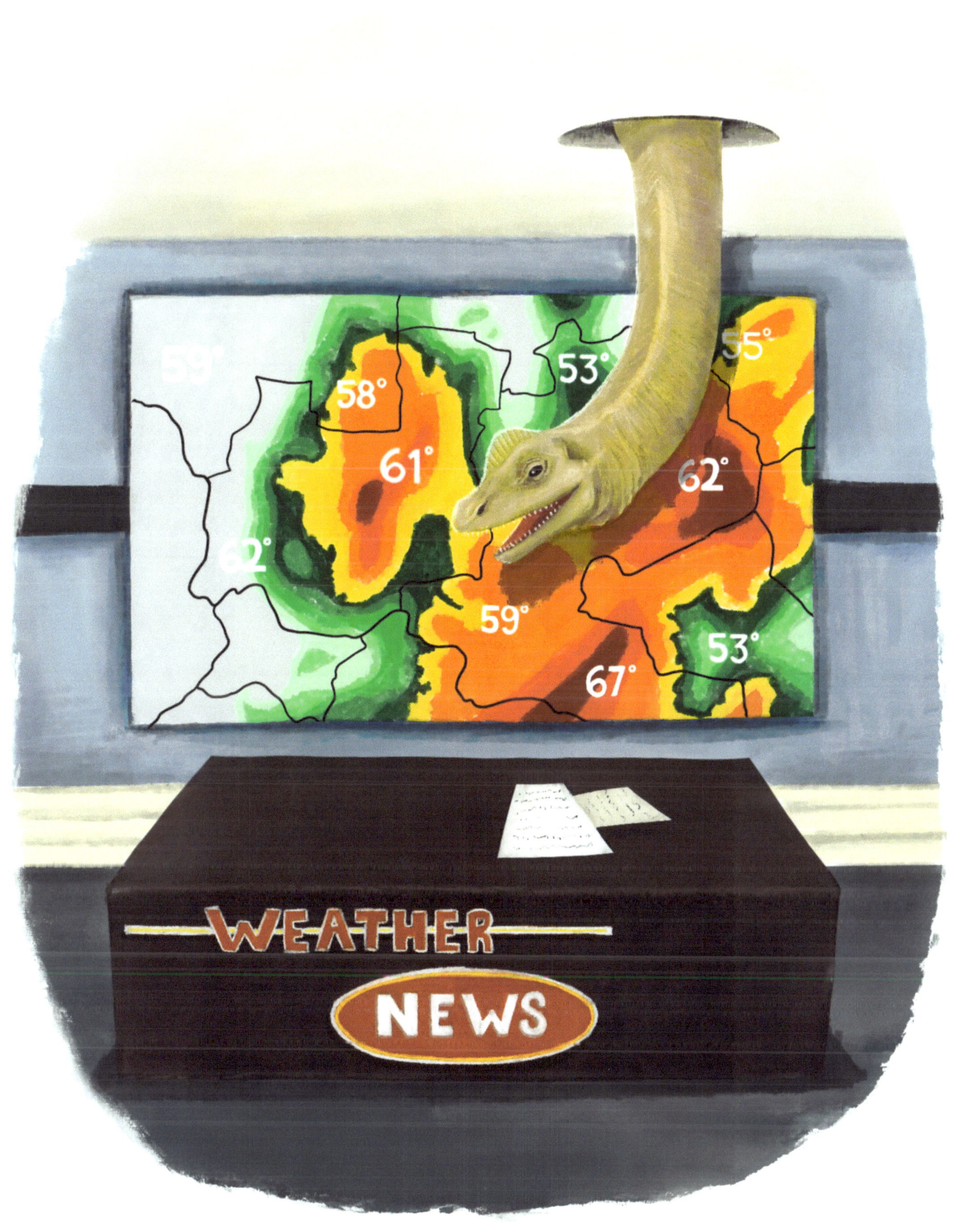
59°
58°
53°
55°
61°
62°
62°
62°
59°
67°
53°
WEATHER
NEWS

The study of plants is what botanists know
They research them closely and see how
they grow

9

These Parasaurolophus
workers collect
Information on traits of
the leaves they inspect

They work in the
greenhouse, the lab, or
outside
And farmers can use what
they learn as a guide

But plants make these
dinosaurs hungry for lunch
Just look at the leaves!
Someone's taken a munch!

These capable chemists
are up to the task
Creating reactions inside
of each flask

13

They wear goggles in case
of a chemical spray
These raptors wear gloves
to be safe everyday!

They understand solids, and
liquids, and gas
And draw out the chemical
models in class

But the board is so high, and
these chemists are small,
To reach it they must stack
up three raptors tall!

CH₃
N
HN
O
N
CH₃
N
C₇H₈N₄O₂
O

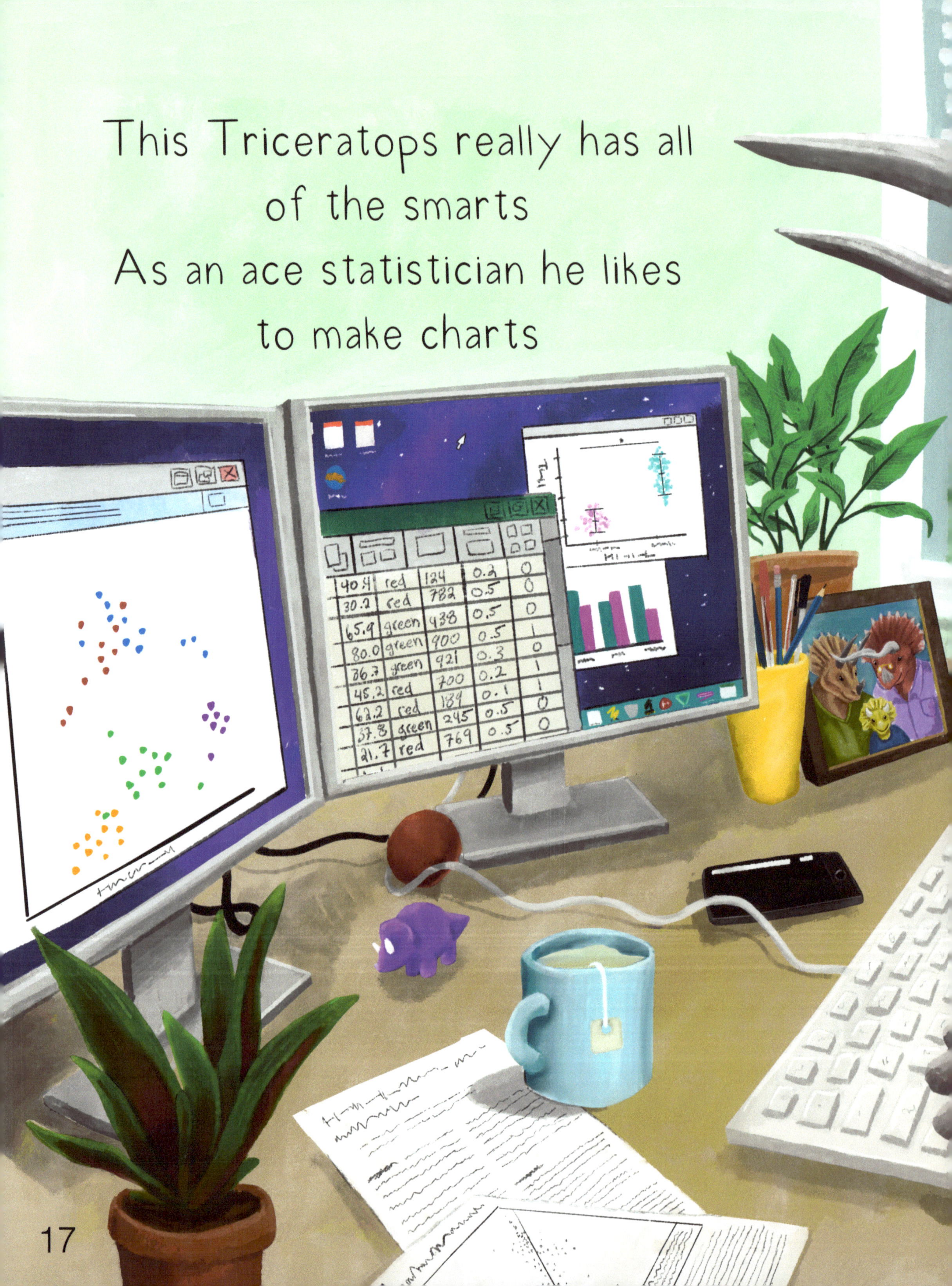

This Triceratops really has all
of the smarts
As an ace statistician he likes
to make charts

He helps with the
numbers that
others collect
And checks that the
answers they get are
correct

He's got skills on
computers, with math he's
so wise
He likes big sets of
numbers of various size

But when he's excited, he
doesn't lean back
His horns hit the screen
and he hears a loud
CRACK!

This paleontologist digs
through the rocks
And places the fossils she
finds in her box
21

This cool Spinosaurus with
shovel and brush
Finds ancient remains that can
easily crush

She studies these creatures
that lived long ago
She places her work in
museums where you go

Her work on display is a great
big success
But look at that mud, she is
making a mess!

NEW FOSSILS!
Ammonite Fossil

These smart neuroscientists study the brain
And all of the quirks that it seems to contain

This Ankylosaurus is running a test
Scanning for brainwaves is what they
do best

They ask questions like,
"Where are our memories
stored?"
And, "What does our brain
look like when we feel bored?"

Just one little problem -
despite their great size,
Most dinosaurs' brains are as
small as their eyes!

Iguanodons study the
forming of stars
These astronomers know
about planets like Mars!

With telescopes
dinos can peer into
space
To learn how the
universe came to
take place

They know how the
planets must circle the
sun
The study of space is
incredibly fun

They help to guide
rockets that blast through
the sky
Let's hope they don't
scare all their friends
they fly by!

Planets of the Solar S
ASTRONOMY

These scientists meet
every once in a while
To share all their research
on posters with style

Each dino's an
expert on subjects
they ace
They each make the
world a more
interesting place

Glossary

Microbiology

The study of tiny organisms called microbes. They are so tiny that we can't see them with just our eyes, so scientists use microscopes to help them work. Microbes live all around us and even in and on us! There are as many microbes on us as cells in our body! Some microbes make you sick (like the flu virus), and some bacteria can make food bad, but many microbes are important for keeping us and our world healthy!

Meterology

The study of the weather. Meterologists learn how hot or cold it will be, how much it will rain and snow, and even how windy it is outside! They use machines to look at the weather all around the planet. One of the fun parts of a meteorologist's job is to report the weather on tv, radio, and online. This lets people know what temperature it is and if it will rain. They can keep people safe by warning them about thunderstorms and tornados.

Botany

The study of plants. There are 390,000 kinds of plants in the world. There are many different kinds of plants. Some are giant trees, some are flowers in a garden, and others make all the fruits and vegetables that you eat. Botanists study how plants grow and how to protect them from bugs that eat them. They also study how to use plants to make medicines for people!

Statistics

A type of math used to help organize all the information that comes from scientific experiments. After running an experiment, a scientist can get a lot of information. For instance, a scientist might measure how tall a plant is every day of the year. If they did this for 100 plants, they would end up with a lot of numbers at the end of the year! Statisticians know just how to organize and look at all these numbers without getting confused. They can make graphs and charts from the numbers that help other people understand too!

Chemistry

The study of all different kinds of matter including liquids like water, solids like rocks, and gases like the air we breathe. There are 118 different kinds of elements and everything in the universe is made up of them, including us! Chemists study how these different elements work together. Using chemistry they can make helpful medicines, fuels, and materials like paints!

Paleontology

The study of plants and animals that lived long ago, before humans existed on the Earth! While paleontologists study many different land and sea animals, the biggest animals they study are dinosaurs, which includes every dinosaur mentioned in this book! Paleontologists find fossils, which are the remains of bones, but can also be imprints that show where a leaf fell or where a dinosaur stepped. Fossils are usually buried in mountains or under water, but paleontologists carefully dig them out and display them in museums so that we can learn about life long ago.

Neuroscience

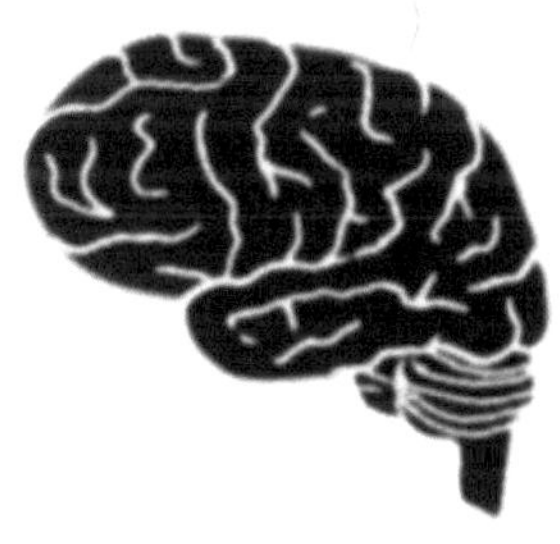

The study of the brain. A brain is an organ in your skull that functions as the control center for your body. Brains help us learn and understand what we see, smell, hear, and touch. It is also the part of our body that has all our feelings, thoughts, and memories. Neuroscientists study everything about the brain, including how we are able to learn and what happens to our brains when we sleep. One way they can understand the brain is by scanning our brainwaves which measures our brain activity!

Astronomy

The study of space including all of the stars, planets, and galaxies that are within it. Astronomers use powerful telescopes and satellites to look very far away so they can see how stars are formed and they can find new planets. Astronomers also use math and physics to understand how objects like planets and comets move in space. This knowledge is very important when planning trips to space and is helpful for engineers who build rockets!

Glossary

Tyrannosaurus Rex (ti-ran-uh-sawr-uhs-reks)
Commonly called a T-Rex, this dinosaur was one of the biggest and strongest meat eaters when it lived 66 million years ago. The T-Rex was over 13 feet tall and over 40 feet long, but its arms were so short that they couldn't reach their own mouth!

Brachiosaurus (brey-kee-uh-sawr-us)
This dinosaur was one of the longest, measuring over 69 feet from head to tail. That is much longer than a school bus! The Brachiosaurus ate plants, and with their long necks they were able to reach leaves on trees over 30 feet tall. Because this dinosaur was so tall it had to have a strong heart to pump blood all around its body. Paleontologists estimate that the heart of a Brachiosaurus weighed 800 pounds!

Parasaurolophus (peh-ruh-saw-raa-luh-fuhs)
This dinosaur could walk on all four legs, as well as just its back two. The Parasaurolophus was an herbivore, meaning that it ate many plants. Its name means "near crested lizard" which refers to the bony crest on top of its head! While scientists are not sure exactly what the Parasaurolophus used its crest for, it may have been used for display or for helping to control its body temperature

Triceratops (trahy-ser-uh-tops)
The name Triceratops means "three horned face". In addition to the three horns on its skull, the triceratops also had a bony frill that helped to protect its neck against attacks from predators, including the T-Rex! Triceratops were strong dinosaurs, measuring 10 feet tall and weighing over 10 tons!

Velociraptor (Vuh-los-uh-rap-ter)

Commonly called raptors, these dinosaurs were very fast! Although Velociraptors were about as small as a turkey, they were feirce predators. They used a large, hooked claw on their hind feet to attack prey. These dinosaurs had feathers and ran on their back two legs.

Spinosaurus (spai-now-saw-ruhs)

The Spinosaurus was semi-aquatic, meaning that it lived both on land and in the water. It was also one of the largest meat-eating predators at over 40 feet long. One of the most prominent features of this dinosaur was the massive sail on its back. It is thought that the Spinosaurus may have used its sail for display or to help control its body temperature.

Ankylosaurus (ang-kuh-low-saw-ruhs)

With thick bony plates lining its back, this dinosaur was built like a tank! At over 20 feet long and weighing up to 8 tons, these bulky dinosaurs were well-protected from predators while they grazed on plants. They also had a thick club at the end of their tail that they could use in defense if needed.

Iguanodon (ih-gwah-nuh-don)

Iguanodons were one of the first dinosaurs discovered! They were herbivores, feeding on a variety of different plants. While they usually walked on all fours, they could stand on their hind legs to reach leaves high up on trees. Iguanodons are also known for their large thumb spikes that they may have used in defense against predators or to help them open fruits and seeds to eat!